I0892566

STILL HUNGRY

STILL HUNGRY

ALISA GORDANEER

George Payerle, Editor

Signature
EDITIONS

Cover design by Doowah Design.
Photo of Alisa Gordaneer by Andrea Scott.

This book was printed on Ancient Forest Friendly paper.
Printed and bound in Canada by Hignell Book Printing Inc.

We acknowledge the support of The Canada Council for the Arts and the Manitoba Arts Council for our publishing program.

Library and Archives Canada Cataloguing in Publication

Gordaneer, Alisa, author
Still hungry / Alisa Gordaneer.

Poems.
ISBN 978-1-927426-64-7 (pbk.)

I. Title.

PS8613.O72S84 2015 C811'.6 C2015-901412-3

Signature Editions
P.O. Box 206, RPO Corydon, Winnipeg, Manitoba, R3M 3S7
www.signature-editions.com

for Kia

CONTENTS

SALT

SOUR

SALT

ARTICHOKE

I cannot love you
if you don't love artichokes.

You have to love thorns. Prickles. You can't doubt
sweetness or draw back before you taste.

I cannot love you
if I can't hold you

cradled in my hands, a steamed spiked blossom
waiting to open. If I can't

dip you in lemon butter,
brush my teeth against your thighs—

devour your sinewed stem,
your soft sharp insides.

SALT

It's best at the edges of tide pools, crystals drying, crusting rocks.
Or in the cellar always on the table, its tiny tarnished spoon

sprinkling conversation: who did what to whom,   why.
Or the heavy grey splinters gravelled between fingers before artichokes.

Remember me then in a blue apron, tossing suspicious white
over my shoulder. It landed on the lino. Considered sweeping—

but instead licked my lips after kissing your distracted forehead:
a gulp of ocean after a sideways wave tastes of accidental skin,

a lick between deep folds, sea flavour
stirred into tea. Transgression lingers:

too much is too much
not enough is not   enough.

EATING DINNER AT YOUR FATHER'S HOUSE

He has never scalloped, sautéed, doesn't
know why anyone would use butter
when margarine is half the price,

has a taste for bacon fat on toast—
palate hardened from years of nothing
but lucky slices of bread.

Still craves tinned meat,
gelatin poised on top when the key peels
back that bright carapace.

Lately we are all hungry from living:
perpetual motion, work and kids, errands and chores.
Exhausted acrobats alighting on each other's fires.

With legs slow and hands shaken,
he has made dinner tonight. Leave that to me
he said. I'll make something good.

Never mind the burned potatoes,
glued gravy, green beans his teeth can chew.
It's four-square on the table. We gather and are fed.

CRUST

Because I am still the one who cleans your shirts,
hangs your socks on the rack

until dryness seeps in. Because I am still the one
kneading bread like I knead

your back, my arms aching late into night. Or because
I am the one who holds you,

cradles and rocks you in my floured arms
even when dawn breaks

pink and you are asleep, my heart beating next to yours and because
you, because me, because we two. Risen

like a loaf of bread in the oven, crusted
before hunger seeps in.

CRACKLING

We have killed spring creatures for dinner.
Irreversible. All we can do now

is honour Lamb. Honour Duck.
Spiced with anise and apricot,

we devour limbs and all. I have baked
sweet bread of lips, tongues.

I would mark your flesh, too, against these dishes.
Take a bite when it is offered, the trace of blood

on your finger enough to scent this meal.
In worship I would stuff your body

roast your flesh to crisp grease,
fill my belly with your unholy name.

OATMEAL EVERY DAY

She's grown used to the feel of oats in her palm,
the right amount and when: a handful now,
then another when the water rolls into boil,
another after stirring and calling children one more time.

Up since five. It used to be easy, the heavy fog of
sleep slipping off with the quilts, the smoke
of dreams clinging as she brushed her hair,
breathed in summer rising in her limbs

but now, under winter, the cool light over the stove
a beacon: this way, this way, follow your own
footsteps every time you stir.
And she wants sometimes to mix it up:

husband and children mumbling in their beds—
she could make history if she pulled on coat
and boots, went out to collect the eggs,
never came back.

It would be trading darkness for light—
until dawn broke and everything
became clear. Her, plodding down a grey road.
She'd want her oatmeal, then.

SLAUGHTERHOUSE

Despite ourselves, we still love meat. Not just fat crisp bellies of pork,
pepper-crusted skins of chicken, but all the squeamish parts:

pink fingers of pork uterus, lamb's kidneys, prairie oysters,
quails' legs no bigger than a thumb,

the lolling lips of cows, webbed feet of ducks,
the white honeycomb of calf's tripe.

We love such transubstantiation, place it on our tongues:
The host says we must eat, and so we may become

redeemed, from red to green:
Their bodies, our bodies. Free-range

taste—not fear of stun gun, knife,
but grass. Through flesh, we ingest the sun.

Under larder floors,
blood still runs.

MARKET/PLACE (DETROIT)

MARKET

Eastern Market's loaded with Saturday morning ghosts: I crave berries and lettuce, peppers, cucumbers, candy-red plums, bushels of tomatoes, Georgia peaches and first corn and shouts: *watermelonwatermelonwatermelonwatermelon* taste it! But there are few vendors in this late blizzard. Snow vortexes across the shed's open floors. I buy flaccid collards, a paper bag of potatoes, a dozen eggs like condensed snowballs. One item from each vendor. A leek. Maple syrup. A purple turnip, skin withered by frost. Steam rises from coffee into a spatter of hail. Dinner will be a confused soup. But pretend abundance, dollars folded into gloves. Today, nobody shouts. An old man asks for spare change and gets a pale Mexicantown tomato instead. He salts it right there. Seeds catch in his beard. A drop of pale juice. *Now that's something,* he says.

PLACE

I drive across the freeway for milk. Park and lock. Slush crusts pavement, the automatic doors stick halfway. Aisles upon aisles. Boxes. Cans. Jars. Food has become cardboard, metal, glass, plastic. Suggested servings with no content, no context. Resemblance/ remembrance gone. Even the meat, a barnyard divided into red, pink, white. Cows recline on Styrofoam, diapered under cling film. Portioned representation, mere slices. Ham-pink, steak-red, chicken skin-wet white. An iridescent trout, its eyes glazed pearl. I think of *Eat up because the starving children,* and *Waste not want not.* And *You are what you eat.* Boxes, cans, jars. Controlled substances. We consume. On a cereal box, happy children play basketball. We can't eat children. Or basketballs. At least there's milk. Gallons of it, white plastic udders stabled in the cold case. And still nothing to eat. An old man asks for change and I want it too. He tells me this: a farm once stood on this site.

PIECES OF CHINA

It's only as I'm polishing the slate tiles newly installed on our kitchen floor
that I stop to think. Ten years of meals and I have dropped more, swept often.

It seems our hopes boil down to masoned stones that can be aligned,
our footsteps measured in square inches, cost assigned per.

I have devised, as one does, ways to smooth rough surfaces, to flavour nights—
cook with sesame oil now, have learned to favour

hoi sin, tamarind, habanero, the sauce we call hot cock. You have
swallowed without comment, and now you walk, sock-footed

across tiles I've rubbed to a dull shine. Actual pieces
of China, carried here. Cemented. Our home has become a shrine.

You open your mouth as if to speak, and I wish for wonder
but instead you tuck in tofu and noodles, sip your wine.

Later, as we're drifting to sleep, you say the kitchen looks different.
What happened, did you sweep?

EGGPLANT

Darling, you've been choosing an eggplant from a cardboard box
beside the market's door, standing for five, ten minutes
mesmerized by thin purple skins, green caps.

Wedged, blocking other shoppers as they pass.
Standing and stooping as though you were kneeling in church
instead of outside Wong's Groceteria in greying half-light.

You're choosing an eggplant from a cardboard box
in late November, when eggplants are scarce and the dark rises
like bruised skin puffed black. It will open into smoke and seeds.

Small-noted music because someone has told you
baba ghannouj is the food for pampered old fathers.
Our bag is already heavy: tahini, garlic, lemons like toys.

Yet you're still choosing an eggplant. Because you want to dawdle
in this flickering doorway, making the overhead bells chime
as life passes in and out.

You're choosing an eggplant to roast until it collapses
inward, like your father's lungs:
indulgence and indulged, rooted in one.

You want to call forth taste where no tastebuds remain.
To do one sacred task: spoon that rough paste
into his still opening, hungering mouth.

SUNDAY DINNER

Anne with a wheat sheaf tattooed between her breasts serves cleavage
over the emptied plates, and the last of the champagne mimics Kate's
jiggle-shimmy—but Kate's like that—and we all giggle after asparagus,
merlot, beef, brie. Yes. Makes you wonder what's happening under
the table when everyone bites into the dessert and sighs over Aunt
Layla's dump cake, all the flour, chocolate, butter and eggs mixed in
the pan like a big old sandbox. Anne says she could recite so many of
those recipes, easy prairie food, potatoes and cream-of-whatever's-
left, but nobody's listening because Kate dances on the table and the
wine glasses tip into puddled napkins. Doubled over, soon someone
is bound to begin her slow slip into disbelief, rail against cheese plates,
ice cream, flesh betrayed—a table the size of Saskatchewan and still
our bellies have room to expand: hunger, that persistent tractor, tills
available, impatient space.

SILVERWARE

I've laid the table as always but now I know
each fork, spoon, knife carries a lover within, lying

composed amid linens and glasses: See, the fork
anticipating its own undulations, tines ever-tease

the spoon, impatient for a thick coat of cream,
rough sugar, smooth fruit. Licking tongues.

Which is why the fork has the jealousy of the jilted,
and the spoon wants nothing more than to bathe in coffee.

So they collude with the knife: everything must be spread.
Tongues will fork, and afterwards, oh, the chatter.

Back in the drawer: whose glossed lips kissed whose
upcurved tines. Who's spooning whom.
Whose handles were grabbed. Or gripped.

CHOKE/CHERRY

I buy a plastic casket of cherries on sale at Whole Foods
because I want to afford an earthly pleasure:

imagine buying a box
of garnets to eat.

My daughter says: you don't eat garnets
but hands me the pitter.

This is for your birthday, I say.
This is a gift.

She is four. And she is happy
as long as I eye the way she is happy,

as long as I place each cherry in the pitter's stirrup,
give birth to a seed wet, bleeding, round.

Months of trying before she fell inside me, a growing tree.
I am mesmerized by pricked fingers, pipettes, garnets.

We poke flesh onto fingertips, fill centers with broken chocolate.
Then bite: inventing heaven in a July kitchen.

Until she insists on eating cherries alone, unpitted. I see stones
rolling like marbles down a long tunnel, looking for somewhere to
stop.

Her throat.
Her breath.

All the summers to come
I'll taste the red of my own lip.

PEARS

It's the unreliability of pears, I think.
The tree bare one year, then broken
branches overladen the next. All that effort.

Until you bite, teeth deep, into their bodies, deceptive.
You might never think such softness
could give beneath that green coat.

It's apparent, such a bottomed-out shape
so vulnerable to puns, to gravity and licking lips
of children who forget to eat the narrow neck.

And that flexing stem, as though it could be
enough in a windstorm, enough to keep fruit
and branch married, wet ground spare of flesh.

BREAKFAST INCLUDED

Fluorescent overheads lean wicked against 6 a.m., Thursday, another day as August ages into what it's owed, one more hot spell before the leaves turn. Sun a yolk in white fog, orange sulfur lamps still humming over the I-89 interchange and the Comfort Inn breakfast room where a too-young grandmother to four girls is letting mama have her shower in peace and quiet, and put that down young lady the baby swatting a plastic spoon into pink Froot-Looped milk. It's all supposed to be a treat, even the cook-your-own waffles poured from plastic cups into the automatic iron, chirping messily. Like the cooler with plastic pots of peach yogurt, blank eyeballs of peeled eggs, factory farming even here where the fields roll rustic into avocado green and harvest gold. A state trooper with the uncanny profile of your absent lover drips three more creamers into Styrofoam. Later, he'll pull you over, won't remember how you stared blankly at the closed-captioned TV, tearful over Lebanon, how you stirred and stirred cup after cup until you just had to leave. How your shaking hands hovered over a brown Formica table where you misplaced a chip of eggshell, he couldn't know how you ached after a night that was, after all, also only a fragment, the whole road between then and now too long to keep driving this fast. How you now know that even sweet time disintegrates, Coffee Mate into a dark cup, enlightenment without substance. How children leave crumbs behind, and you, weeping with a crumpled napkin, sweeping up.

SOURDOUGH STARTER

What is made and consumed, made again:
our hands pushing bread dough, flour dust
starred across the tabletop   this wood worn
because all our mouths open, moan *hungry*.
Where did it all start? The ferment reaching back
to mother, grandmother, great-ancestor
until we fade. Imagine us all in line
waiting, since beginnings, microscopic
yeast born and consumed, reborn in the same
bread, new every day. Be here now, with me.
While we toss old crusts to the fire, small remnants rise.

DINNER IS BURNT

Of course I am at fault, a fact unspoken, but we all know
it's due to crucial, unrestrained elements. You still assign blame.

Dinner would never burn if I were more attentive,
could put down that book, drop my pen—

remember who I am married to
and act.

And yet, when the roast is secure in the oven, I forget
to check until blackened flesh sears—

How could I? Sustenance should be nurtured like all good
things: the peas from the garden. A home. Our children, for Pete's sake.

Everyone will starve if I am in charge for much longer,
so I plan to abdicate. I know what's in store.

I should be ashamed. Dinner is ruined
and I have written recipes for escape.

BANNOCK

Bread bakes now, and I already write to you, describing the dough
and how I couldn't trust its body, the same as I can no longer trust my own.

In another few hours, you will catch a ferry home, feel the ocean swell.
You will shout what's left unsaid to the flying air, shout

about what will become of us. Crusts we no longer want, dried and blackened.
Our bodies no longer wanted: desire rehearses, but no curtains rise.

I draw a five-pointed star to guide you away from me, because you will take
the most difficult route, and need alternate directions.

Otherwise, you'll never find your way back again—
you'll build a fire in a ring of rock, hoist twisted dough above all.

Outside your embrace, I burn and burn.
In the end you will follow the smell of baking bread.

SOUR

PLUM JAM

Everything is different this year
but jam still needs to be made
because red plums are thudding onto grass.

We celebrate, marking summers.
The year we added lemon. The year it didn't jell
and we poured it over ice cream until we couldn't eat.

You send the children out with pails, and their
arms strain against ripeness. Last year they were too small,
pushed plums into their own mouths.

This year, everything too much to contain:
garden overgrown, trees weighed down,
wasps drunk. Bees drowsy with boozy juice.

In the hot kitchen, I slice out pit after pit.
The big pot simmers, scent bittersweet.
You pull glass jars from the oven, sterile,

then ladle jam, pretending there is no such thing as news,
that I haven't said what I couldn't keep
from bubbling over:

Nothing is safe.
Not the jars in the cellar,
unopened from last summer.
Not the day, not this earth or
the children humming with pleasure in the yard.

You offer me a
spoon, sticky with jam.
I have no taste for red turning pale.

JUST DESSERTS

I have baked your sweets for much too long,
these half-pitted cherries, my hands stained red
for clafoutis, cherry pie, cobbler, crumbles
I've offered up sweetly, like nothing is wrong.

These half-pitted cherries, my hands stained red,
honeyed in your presence, I sour when you're gone.
I've offered up sweetly, like nothing is wrong,
with cream, whipped cream, vanilla ice cream,

honeyed. In your presence, I sour. When you're gone,
you make my jutting bones eat more
with cream, whipped cream, vanilla. I scream.
Should I follow a quick, tart recipe for hate?

You make my jutting bones eat more
exotic ingredients you'll never sample.
Should I follow a quick tart recipe for hate,
I'll turn up the heat, stir in some trouble.

Exotic ingredients you'll never sample
for clafoutis, cherry pie, cobbler, crumbles.
I'll turn up the heat, stir in some trouble:
I have baked your sweets for much too long.

NO MORE DESSERT

I sat at the dinner party, crumpled children in the living room
craving their beds, and demolished chicken in the kitchen
a carcass laid out on its rumpled bed of rice. Under the
thin scent of herbs, the thick scents of wine and
chocolate hung in the air, oh look, guests so vivid
in their satin and silk. I noticed their small hand
movements, their lips opening and closed, and
how we were all so alive. How this evening
was a banquet unto itself, and the clink of
cutlery, the glasses, the spiked merry hell
of broken stemware on the floor when
we bent awry in laughter. It was just
so very human, then, and why at
the same moment as I thought
all was still, perfect within,
it was time, yes, time, and
the coats were lifted off
the hostess's bed and
we slow-bundled.
There was no
more dessert
no more
yes, no.
No.

A MAN WHO BAKES

In the field, crows perch
on pumpkins: black seeds scattered
against mist, mud, old hungers

It's the grey season and we all crave orange—
crows know
an ending when they taste it

So I tell you this, last ditch:
nothing is more seductive
than a man who bakes

That's when you cobble a pie:
press crust, and crush pumpkin flesh

Bake it lopsided   too soft to cut

WE DON'T GET ALONG IN THE KITCHEN

as I find out over the smudged counter:
you crave rare steak while I marinate tofu.

You have fire on your mind
but there are only two burners.

I plan salad and bread—
you manage to scorch both.

I should have known:
Your knives are never sharp,

the counter unwiped between mealtimes,
the silverware black-tipped

and the crumbs!
Floors pebbled with them.

I'm not complaining.
I still want to feed you, starving bear,

save you the best morsels.
Always wish for growth,

even as I watch you pour green olive oil
into the carafe, then pungent sweet balsamic.

The oil rises, a green bubble. I sink into vinegar:
too many dishes, broken and whole, left to do.

PEPPERMINT

The house guests are gone, taking their empties
and leaving the keys you loaned. It has been

three days, everything quiet now.
I imagine you can hear yourself think at last:

salt water rushing in ears, heart
pushing another hot pint. Imagine you still feel

the way she, in the kitchen, laced her fingers through yours, a look
and then turning, her own husband in the next room. You must have heard

him laugh too loud when I said something funny and (you suspect)
embarrassing, though you deny that now.

It's been three days.
You still feel her hands in yours.

The kitchen cleaned, newspapers folded. I want to go shopping;
the sales are on and it's the weekend. You nod, eyes fixed on tired tinsel.

It will be January before the tree is down, needles on the floor and
catching in your socks. You'll appreciate the pricks then, having become one

or so I will say. Even after three weeks, nothing given
will be returned. I'll bet you can't stop thinking: Those fingernails

painted red and white, each a peppermint
found unwrapped.

CHICKEN SIMMERS

Chicken simmers.
Mood grows grimmer.

Dishes clatter,
nothing matters.

Dinner half done,
gulped on the run:

your lips' loud smack,
your hunched-over back.

You barely taste
in your made-up haste.

You couldn't mind
if I were less kind.

Everything matters.
Everything shatters.

After you ate
I threw a plate.

STALEMATE

Nothing's left. I learn the bad news over good merlot
and unremarkable dinner, fraught with pieces of shell and cavernous want:

the muse has quit. Up and left with no trace,
a body turned away, a disappointed lover's back faced at night.

No longer hungry, I feed magpies who skip, peck, sample
what shines, what glitters, what reflects. They'd rather eat the sun.

Consider fight or flight: in the kitchen, you knock dishes in the sink
until something breaks. Eggs shattered in tonight's omelet, us still not full.

How can I hunger for this? Even the bread grows hollow,
yeast over-risen, bubbling into empty spaces. No food assembles here.

Crumbs dry in my mouth. I taste the stale-
mate. Blackbirds no longer sing. The wine is gone.

RAW

I don't want to taste anything until it's cooked. Like wearing a shirt
before its buttons are sewn, or its collar attached. You, though,

are impatient, bite ragged slices of carrot, torn cabbage,
a whole red pepper. Seeds falling into your hand.

A slice of tuna rests on the green plate, pink
as the inside of your cheek. To do this right

I know the knives need sharpening. I whet
stones and appetite.

I have kissed someone else and you know. You lean against the counter,
grip your wine glass, tap. One. Two. Three. Four.   Silence.   Again.

This isn't cooking, I say, fumbling edges into sharpness
until I grasp ways to separate everything   from everything else.

BESIDES THE CAKE

My sister decided not to stay married
after just three hours

her fondant dress slumped in August heat,
translucent taste of champagne lingering on her tongue—

after all those pecked cheeks and photographs, too many
sweaty arms, backs, too many hugs and all she wanted

was to slide unseen like a knife into a cool white
tundra of icing,

to bury what was.
The catered salmon cold on rented china,

her borrowed groom outside in the dark,
smoking, still.

SESAME

You rubbed sesame oil on your work-chapped hands
until you smelled like a take-out order of noodles
eaten quickly in a Metro car. Before you disappeared like the train itself,

I sprinkled sesame seeds on vegetables, each grain adding suspense.
I wanted to taste your fingerprints on each asparagus stem, and the thin
slip of blood you thought I didn't see, your cracked finger so quickly to your lips.

I wanted to write a love poem for your hands, before the scent of sesame
became bound with heat and summer, melting into subways,
the whoosh of what was, and what vanished.

I still smell sesame when dinner is gone, the dishes washed
and stowed in cupboards. What was ordered
was perfect, you said. And opened the door.

AT THE SAME TIME

as she whisks the eggs she's pouring stock
melting butter adding sugar adjusting flavour greasing
pans setting temperature beating batter kneading
dough dropping by spoonfuls deglazing salting sweetening
spicing shaking. Shouting for the kids, noticing their hems rising,
searching for homework sharpening pencils
negotiating between, on behalf of, before, because—and calling, cajoling
caressing, convincing. Setting the table, slicing bread. Chilling wine.
And listening for the car, licking lips tasting dressing nudging
a curl behind her ear, her reflection into the glasses. Biting her lip.
And at the same time a robin chirrups a raven calls
the bus roars by the phone rings
time slows her heart beats blood pumps cake rises
sauce thickens bread browns onions caramelize.
Her children want their dinner. Their father won't arrive.

GREEN BEANS

She's wearing my shoes and sleeping in my bed
with my husband, so it goes without saying

she shouldn't also be in my vegetable garden,
harvesting the green beans I planted in June,

even if summer's failing, and the leaves aching into red.
Her hands are stained by the half-bushel already harvested.

She'll argue with him, like I have, about stems.
Heads or tails no longer a matter of winning.

So she'll take the ends to the compost and carry
sunflowers back to my green vase.

Cut the stems on angles;
they'll lean softer against my eyes.

SAVING SUMMER

Abundance, the word lyric
and bellied
abounding.

Harvest of clingstones
bottled like specimens,
the big chest freezer a morgue

of red berries,
beheaded chickens,
trout caught and iced.

I say   it's for winter, when trees rise
bereft and the mouth
unfull.

You say
                        I can't
                        let go.

AFTER THE FLOOD

Separating eggs, one has to be agile: one small
slip and the whole meringue's ruined. Which could be why

we're walking on eggshells today, why the devil
has fucked the angel cake.

You lurk beside me, next to the oven you
turned up to 450 degrees. It's going to burn like that.

I tell you there is no other way to restore lightness
but to start again, let each egg divide

in its own raw time, let the slick message of albumen
slide clear of the muddying yolk.

Yes, love, it's hard to let go,
but sometimes nothing else works: after the flood

of yellow, the heartbreak of omelets again—
and no dessert.

GANACHE

Nobody eats the icing, do they? Unless
they're very hungry, don't care about weight
or can't get enough sugar because it's

the last good thing. Unless they are left alone
in a chilly kitchen with slices cut
and the party over—

those measured portions lined up
can-can dancers practising
a triangular mockery:

Tell me. Who sang *happy birthday* loudest, darling?
Who waited until their wishes were gone
before blowing out the lights?

LEMONS

I'm eating half lemons soaked in gin when you say
you are leaving. Everything sinks into bitter,

past the naïve pledge of wedding vows
to the deep bottom of my glass,

words left on my rimed tongue. Defeat,
wrinkled and warm like, well, half a lemon soaked in gin.

The kids are out watching the Perseids, their eyes widened with darkness
and the news. An enormous sharp taste you no longer stash in your pocket.

I still carry their baby teeth with my coins, to snap at me when I fish for change.
Like biting a lemon, inevitably coming up sour.

What's next, then?
A glass of gin and lemon, brined, spat away.

BUTTERMILK

She says, pouring buttermilk into her chipped mug,
that cats know everything about
substance. About mist. About
places between fingers where skin

and sinew meet.
That women know whatever can be
known about systems, promises,
men and women.

How to stay warm.
To fill the belly with something
you could sip.
Thick and sour, a morning kiss.

BITTER

OBSESSED

we sip water or coffee (black) but funny how food has come up
in conversation   at last count ten times   eleven   twelve

and yet to the waiter's frustration we've declined
toast eggs bagels even salad is a provocation

not just yet
or *maybe later*
or *I'm still choosing*
it all looks so good I just can't decide…

but we won't
because around the table   menus down   taboos up—

not eating today
not hungry now

oh   not hungry   no
don't eat until five

don't eat until dark
don't eat   if I can help it

starving women
telling lies

turn away the man
with impatient eyes

DESERVE

she tells me so often she sees the word *serve* in *deserve*
and its severe lines scored against what must   always   be refused

late night on Granville Street   yobbos shouting from the pub
the Canucks are losing   she's hungry for company

more than food   but what's the harm?   a single
chocolate bar   one more French fry   resist

resist again   to give in is surrender
such determined loins to gird   fronts to keep up

one yob calls himself Sir Dave   kisses her hand
buys her lite beer   she hates its piss-water taste

but he is hilarious   says his whole town went on a diet once it was on TV
and all   only he skipped out   chowing down in Hope

she suspects he's hinting at something
declines the nachos even though … salt-crunch …

for one night   she deserves cheese
a green spike of jalapeno   one bite   just one bite

excuses   in the ladies'   she touches
finger to throat   it doesn't take long

when she returns
the plates   and Dave   are gone

WASTE

I will no longer participate   you say
                    pushing the full plate to table's edge
no amount of guilt can change the world
                    nothing taken   *nothing left*
six hundred pounds of food a year each
                    into the trash   disposer   landfill
in Sudan   Ethiopia   Uganda   elsewhere
                    children die with swollen bellies
still   we choose the nicest peaches   tempting plums
                    apricots wrinkle on the counter
untouched

avoid: restaurants, cafes, food courts, bistros, greasy spoons.
drink: lemon juice, maple syrup and cayenne pepper in water. every day—

ELIMINATION DIET*

(*a controlled experiment)

what's safe:

rice
apples
water

what's not safe:

asparagus, avocado, artichokes, almonds, bananas, berries, bagels, beef, blood sausage, bacon. and cinnamon, cardamom, cumin, cilantro, carrot, coffee, chicory, cannelloni, cannoli, cayenne, curry, collards, cheese. donuts, deer, daikon, duck, eggplant, eggs, flour, farina, fennel, farfalle, filberts, goosefat, grease, grapes, guava, horseradish, ice cream, jalapeno, jicama, kohlrabi, kale, lemon, lime, lutefisk, marjoram, mace, mushrooms, milk, nutmeg, noisettes, onions, oranges, octopus, olives, pineapple, pork, potatoes, peppers, pizza, peanuts, peaches, pears, quince, rabbit, radish, shrimp, salmon, soursop, turnip, thyme, tamarind, udon, umeboshi, vanilla, waffles, xanthan, xigua, yams, yogurt, zucchini. zabaglione.

like breath, moving in. moving out.
like your own mind.
like your own sense.

unanticipated reaction: all foods become impossible. every bite
risks sullen potential.

what's safe:

____
____
____

the process of elimination
eliminates.

(*an uncontrolled result)

a kitchen with nothing in it but water
a banquet at which everyone is eating but you

DIETARY

if one piece of bread then no cheese: if cheese
one piece only and no orange: if orange, have two
(because cheese is orange but orange is fruit)

cauliflower is free. a whole head of broccoli
is worth a day off because you'll need it
after all that green chewing. try this:

lying on your back, massage the stomach,
left to right, a giant letter c. you are describing
yourself as you will become after—

if salad, you can cheat. eat double, fill up
with greens. then fried chicken, chocolate,
mile-high-lemon-pie: nothing counts

if you eat dessert first, you satisfy. think
of calories going in, small creatures
living inside.

if one piece of day, no night. if night, one day
you will be right
to say you're full   then, and only then

you may push that plate away.

NOT HUNGRY

appetite lost. gone.
cravings diminish, vanish:
swallow only light.

starvation, you know
grows such elegant fingers,
such wide-open eyes.

RULES

there are lots:
a single cup of black coffee, followed by a boiled egg
one can of tuna for lunch, with lemon juice. or no lunch
slice a bagel in three, eat only two parts. tomorrow just the third
divide the plate. fill the smallest quarter. take away half
drink a glass of water before every meal
a glass of water is a meal
breathe fresh air on waking. live on that

body grows slender, mind clarifies
shake your head: the waiter brings just a chilled glass

RICE

spoon contains: rice   plain white   long grain
enumerate 79
grains
eat them all   one by one
/
/
/
/
/
/
/
/
/
more
than enough

learn this joke:

                    mind
                    matter

say it again
place the spoon beside the plate

a face upside down and thin

sublimation
substantiation

FAST

first thing to know:

it isn't

one lasted 63 days the record 94
not all end on purpose

any hunger artist knows:

it could go on could

transcend even death.

look: your closed mouth.
look: your dry eyes.

believe this:

if you eat it will kill you.
if you don't eat it will kill you.

the only question:

speed.

(WARNING: MAY CONTAIN)

a sense of daring once you conquer the initial shock of pepper
or a harmless tingle of carbonation, naturally fermented
a gung-ho dollop spiked with a dab of regret
the leftovers, yet to be dealt with, cooling on the counter
rocky pits sticking between your teeth and your tires
more than one ingredient ending in -ide
more than one cheese ending in -zola
some measure of commitment required for caramel only
a masala of ten spices you must blend or ignore
a warning from those who have gone before: take small bites first
jackfruit   mangosteen   quince
your own body changed

hipbones connected directly to the headbone
you look great *he says* I like your blouse how it hangs

LIVE ON

still   you deny/
                defy

but what if you had to live on
grasshoppers? eyes faceted, clinging sticks in amber grass
or limpets prised from shore rock. raw, their rubbery feet
scavenged blackberries, not yet ripe, a sour red shock
or blue camas bulbs in springtime. only in spring
if there were nothing else: slugs, roasted over fire
if there were something else: salal berries, oysters, clams
if that were all
would you
live on?

ribs corrugate your skin
even the moonlight fills you up

WHAT YOU WILL EAT

in autumn, your bowl of squash soup and a dipping spoon   you
could ask for nothing more   just this   and a piece of bread

angled light turns leaves to crumbs   we are getting older
bodies slowing as the children catch up   it's colder these days

as though the sky could draw its own heat from your hands
which is why you clutch this bowl   and why the orange soup

disappears into your mouth so slowly   you are savouring the
flavour of endings   love   you scrape the last few drops of warm

do you know what you will eat
when the light is gone?

SOMETIMES IT'S ENOUGH

with fingers closing on orange peel, scent
of oil rising, hungry now for the first time

since the driveway's flagstones cracked beneath the weight
of the moving truck. one last load, then silence. he didn't wave.

didn't call that night, the dust in the corners
tracing question marks. the cat purred, though,

and at night nobody crept down to see what those noises were
so she curled into pillows, and now I can say she wept

as each segment of orange weeps its own story of sweet, or tart.
sometimes it's enough to fill a mouth with another's song.

enough to sit and watch the sisterhood of ants
carry fragments of peel across hot stones.

SWEET

BREAKING THE FAST

After weeks of abstinence, we eat again.
Anything will do, hunger become so brittle

you could break it with dirt, with stones, with
rutabaga. It wouldn't matter. Your maniacal

dinner fork poised, all this eagerness
for a slice of bread. We've toasted it, spread

the last of the butter, divided it between us
with a ruler and the only sharp knife left.

We've talked all day about this moment,
anticipated triangles on the chipped green plate.

You let me choose while you turn away, light a candle:
illuminate these caves, our open mouths.

EATING CROW

We would, if it came to that.   Not that it will.   I imagine
other animals are more easily caught

before we scoop sooty wings from the sky
into our hungry embrace.

Bunnies, for example. Or squirrels. We'd dare chew their tiny legs
before we'd pluck black feathers and deep-fry crow drumsticks.

But if we were hungry enough
we'd pull off wings, roast crows over a dwindling fire.

We would.   And we both know it, the crow and I, eyeing
each other over the rail of the back balcony.

What would he taste like? Black licorice. Nori. Currants glossed with night.
Murder, my love, would taste all right.

PEELED

The night before your surgery, we slice peels
from apples until the floor is scattered red.

You joke about scalpels, skin, slices
not knowing what will happen

when you are there
but not.   It's the moment of enforced stillness

and the deep-breathed counting back from 10
that makes you nervous, more than the time

you climbed up the birch
to see if you could reach the apple

tree's full limbs. That's what set this whole
thing in motion: your body sliding downwards

like an unripe apple
the way you landed and looked up

blinking, your mouth opening and closing:
you were trying to explain the meaning of saints.

You were singing praise
to an untaken bite.

STILL HUNGRY

As always in September I wake
in sloping peach-yellow mornings and remember
there have been too few peaches this summer

know that as many furred skins as have prickled my lips,
as many slick crevices as have fallen beneath your teeth,
there have never been enough.

The sun lowering like overripe fruit is only a reminder,
and so is the moon grown pregnant and gold,
and the baskets of pumpkins where once were peaches

just moments ago. As always in September—
and yet the days lean into winter and far away
I know I'll wish for jam

but I spent the season
lingering in your arms, feeding you peaches,
sure (then) that winter would feel as warm.

POLLO CON CHILI

You are learning peppers, small bites at first,
easily licking the challenges
of jalapeño, serrano, habanero. Now you can tease
flavour into so many pores, even alter the way you breathe.

You string a bushel of Thai reds on black thread,
a garland grown from earth and market stalls.
They sound like chickens, clucking as they're hoisted, feet up
in peppery autumn light.

Nerves still move until the heart stops:
Like humans parting ways, they still flail
when their heads are severed.
Blood runs bright.

But you say it's all right:
they, unlike us, feel no pain.
I say drown them in chilis.
Let them feel again.

SOUP

You've made soup from roots again, craving the earth
and a sense of gallows humour.

Gravely, I sense excellent bones in this stock, today
know a body rooting in the darkness for a place to grow.

Have you ever looked for mandrake? For wild carrot,
the flesh of all things fingering deep in their quest to become?

Can you hear buried bones growing into trees, the ribcages
of elm and poplar begging the sky just to breathe?

It's a question of soup, you say: nothing more, just the careful parings
of daily need, shed into a bowl as each night melts over Earth.

You crave this soup, this substance, this wet. Want to carry it
in a clay bowl, spoon akimbo, trying not to spill.

HOUSESITTING

I want to bake something and leave it
waiting for your return, something with
chocolate or rum, a greeting
to press between your lips.

In your hollow kitchen,
I taste sugar from the bowl, sustain hope with nothing
more than a hint of melon,
grapes, rosemary—

move small objects as though to say I was here—
a fading bundle of narcissus in a vase, your poetry
books ajar, the new carton of eggs.
A plum pie in the fridge, with only a few bites gone.

HOT SAUCE

You're crazy they said, but it was summer-crazy
the kind that comes after a day in hundred-degree heat
and gets hotter like a bug under the beam
of a magnifying glass because we've cracked a few cold
ones, got a few hot ones watching. It was only a matter
of time before the hot sauce met the ice cream
only a matter of time before that cold and that hot
met our lips and cooled and burned at once
only a matter of time before we were kissing the summer
with all our might licking up vanilla with a hint
of habanero, the cooling night an ice cube down our backs
and oh how we could dance oh how hot
it was your skin like vanilla the sky
velvet overhead and lifting slowly off like my dress
that got just a little too tight the crazy clinging heat
and us tasting hot sauce in our kisses hot sauce beer
vanilla the flavours of summer in our crazy laughing mouths.

RASPBERRY PIE

for Andrew and Sylvie

You bake raspberry pie with your daughter
because there is now desire at work in both of you. You write *want*
with your fingers, drifted sugar on the wooden counter.

Those berries have ripened in the time she's slipped from girl to woman:
pale crust of skin tanned with summer, freckles sprinkled,
eyes bright as your new pans.

It's also new to you, this recipe:
Your common ground found over a bowl of softening berries,
words sugared

to explain your work in this kitchen, warm
with August night and baked cinnamon:
what you'll both become.

You stand surprised when the pie is crisped,
stop yourself when she giggles at your ragged slices,
reach for a pair of plates and settle down to something good.

Because what you know, now, is everything.
What she knows, now,
is everything else.

SATURDAY

Despite the rest of this week I am in love with Saturday,
all the sleeping-in-flapjacked-happiness of maple morning

and coffee, oh! That third jazzed cup with extra cream
and almond liqueur before noon, lingering

over papers rumpled on the table where sunshine streams
across headlines of nothing consequential, the day

stretched out towards evening: a cat
in the armchair, waiting to pounce—

PICNIC

Bring the bottles of wine from the cellar, reds
and whites forgotten under dust. Bring the
glasses, too, rubbed clean with linen. Bring love.

Bring the olives, slick with salt and oil,
the taste of hot days far away. Bring the
artichokes, asparagus, avocadoes, everything from the beginning

and bring the creamy brie, the creamy blue, the creamy skinned
camembert knowing it will stick on my face.
Bring the beginnings of conversations, bring

the cloth we've carried since the first
day of marriage, the gift meant to be spread
on grass, sand, unfurled like a flag. Bring it

because we haven't used it in years, bring the wrinkled
fibre and the faded roses
and the fraying edges.

Bring these small things, and bring the intent to lie
on this green hill and tell me, again, with water and wine that you will
bring bread, too—

and yams, and zucchini.
And if you can't bring food,
bring love.

LEFTOVERS

After dinner: joyous bones, exhausted
salad. The bottle of brandy we'll finish in bed.

Candles, stalactite-thin, and our lashes burnt wicks,
fingers tapering into bone-white glisten.

We need no pie to sweeten this moment:
words on your tongue an ellipsis of pips.

I want to kiss that scar on your shoulder,
want to remind our skins we've finally healed.

We will leave this table. I will lead you
to sample what remains unserved.

STARVATION IS FAR AWAY

from the story you told of the man who worked in a cheese shop,
stuffed 300 grams of marscapone down his pants. Asked his lover
to lick it from his cracker. You know. You were there.

And far away from duck fat, goose grease,
bacon fat hardened in the fridge and spread on toast.
From bacon itself. I love that we can eat bacon, now.

Far, too, from asparagus sprouting in unexpected places,
gathered in springtime for frivolous dishes.
This is what we do when there is more than enough.

From a New York strip loin cooked rare, in butter.
When we knew what it was to be animal
and famished and devoured.

From the first apple ripe on the new tree.
I had wanted to cut it into six pieces, give everyone a bite.
You got there first, munched it while you raked the leaves.

From the box of mangoes I bring to our kitchen, forgetting your allergies.
The children slice the halves into porcupines, paint their faces yellow
with juice. And scrub their cheeks pink so you can kiss them goodnight.

From bread, the way you showed me how to make it, letting it rise
in the cold. I think of you every time I grab a fistful of chilled dough,
every time it warms into loaves, bakes up crisp and hot.

From caramel, chocolate, crème brûlée, clafoutis.
From egg white. How it hardens into melting crispness.
From the way whipping cream peaks into clouds.

From the chipped blue bowls we washed
and washed again.
From the way they stayed empty, but now are full.

HOG'S HEAD

We've never thought of heads as having heft
but you need to drop the shopping bag onto pitted concrete, rest

beside the apple stall a moment, bite slices of crisp spartan, smile thanks
to the curvy Armenian woman who sells us three for a dollar.

Today we choose red apples for their skins, imagine how they'll look in the
pig's maw. We chose a hog's head because low-brow magic must be worked.

In its bag, blind blue eyes accuse. You arrange the handles,
then strain your arm with that weight. You were warned.

The farmer double-bagged without asking, charged per pound.
Plastic ridges your fingers white.

Tonight, when we are alone in the kitchen with the head of a pig,
we'll remember it's not about magic, or voodoo, or recipes anymore.

You'll grasp its ears, fold back the moist snout,
trace the pale lips cautiously, a lover with smiling jowls, elegant jaw.

You'll finger an apple, too, because it will fit there,
as would your fist.

I stand by your cauldron, surprised again. The weight
of my head, too filled to stir.

ACKNOWLEDGEMENTS

"Oatmeal Every Day" appeared in *Alimentum Magazine,* Issue 9, Winter 2010. New York.

"Cherry" appeared as "Garnets" in *With a Cherry on Top: Stories, Poems, Recipes and Fun Facts from Michigan Cherry Country* (ed. Angela Williams, Mayapple Press, Bay City MI, 2006)

"Green Beans," "Breakfast Included," "Sunday Dinner," "Eating Crow," and "Besides the Cake" appeared in *Grain Magazine,* Fall 2011.

"What You Will Eat" appeared in *Framing the Garden,* ed. Linda Rogers, Ekstasis Press, 2011

"Stalemate" appeared in *Carte Blanche,* Issue 12, May 2012

"Eggplant," "Market/Place" and "Elimination Diet" appeared in *PRISM International,* 51:2, Fall 2012.

This book was made possible through the support of the Canada Council for the Arts, the Banff Centre, and the Vermont Studio Centre, all of which provided me with time, funding and excellent nutrition while I worked on these poems. I am immensely grateful for these organizations' dedicated nourishment of the arts.

Jan Zwicky's comments on early drafts of this book helped leaven, spice and salt it. Carolyn Forché encouraged me to try a few new recipe ideas. I owe a special thanks and more than a few homecooked dinners to John Barton, who's added much more than a soupçon of wine, and many pastries to my excellent editor, George Payerle, who played Iron Chef to make something tasty of this book.

And then there are those who keep my head filled: Magritte Gordaneer, Miria and Jim Gordaneer, and also Sacha Christensen and Marc Christensen. Margot Mackay taught me a thing or two about cooking with fire. The Wildwood Writers, especially Kari Jones, Julie Paul and Laurie Elmquist, provided tea and cookies that never failed to fuel and inspire. Coffee, IPA and hot sauce contributed, and too much MSG caused heartburn. Robert Swereda arrived in time to keep the whole dish from burning. Thanks to all.

ABOUT THE AUTHOR

Alisa Gordaneer is a poet, writer and editor who has taught at the University of British Columbia, the University of Victoria, Camosun College and Royal Roads University. She has worked as a newspaper editor, communications consultant and freelance journalist, writes regularly for Victoria's *CVV Magazine*, and serves on the board of the Creative Nonfiction Collective Society. A member of the League of Canadian Poets, she has won many awards for her poetry and nonfiction.

Eco-Audit

Printing this book using Rolland Opaque 30 instead of virgin fibres paper saved the following resources:

Solid Waste	Water	Air Emissions
20 kg	1,611 L	181 kg